Classical Guitar Favorites

SHEET MUSIC AND VIDEO INSTR

T0085223

Cherry Lane Music Company
Director of Publications/Project Editor: Mark Phillips
Project Coordinator: Rebecca Skidmore

To access video, visit:
www.halleonard.com/mylibrary

Enter Code
3823-2678-8345-1445

ISBN 978-1-60378-314-9

Visit Hal Leonard Online at
www.halleonard.com

World headquarters, contact:
Hal Leonard
7777 West Bluemound Road
Milwaukee, WI 53213
Email: info@halleonard.com

In Europe, contact:
Hal Leonard Europe Limited
1 Red Place
London, W1K 6PL
Email: info@halleonardeurope.com

In Australia, contact:
Hal Leonard Australia Pty. Ltd.
4 Lentara Court
Cheltenham, Victoria, 3192 Australia
Email: info@halleonard.com.au

Bouree in E Minor

Johann Sebastian Bach

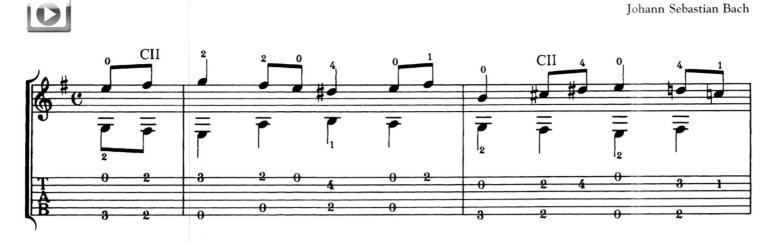

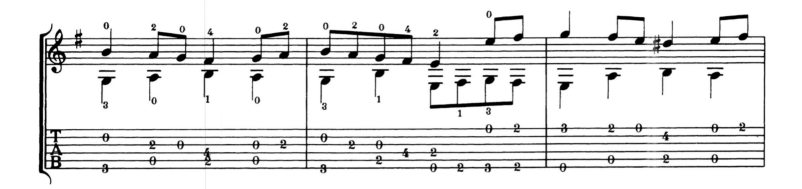

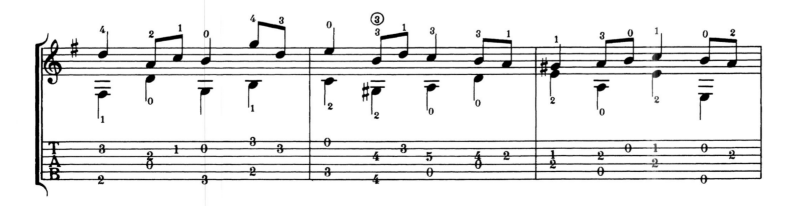

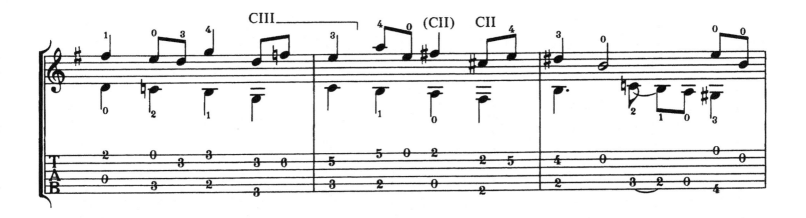

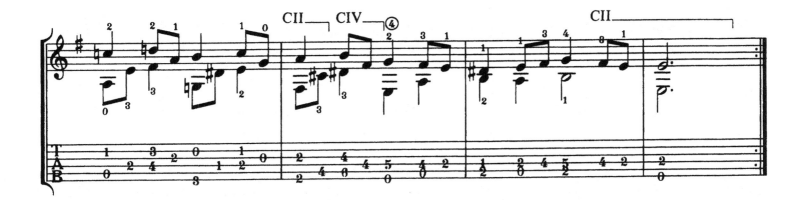

3

Jesu, Joy of Man's Desiring

Johann Sebastian Bach

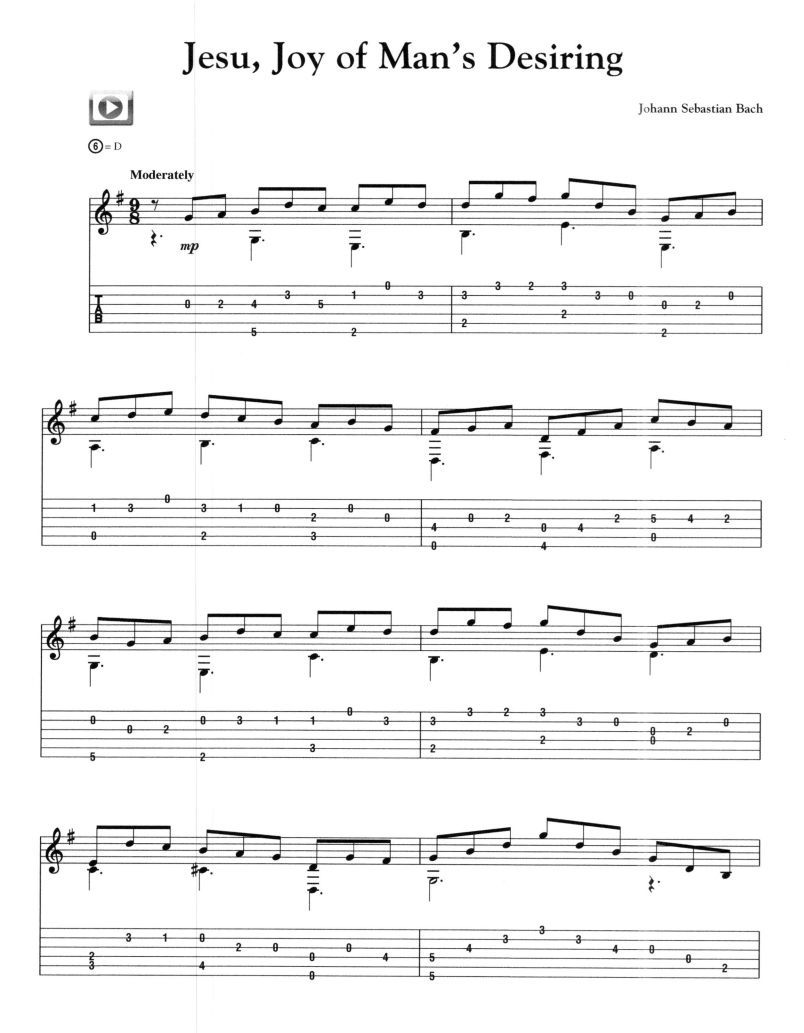

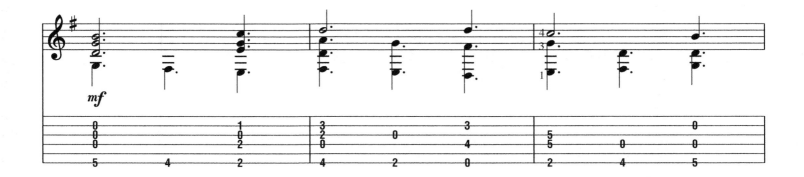

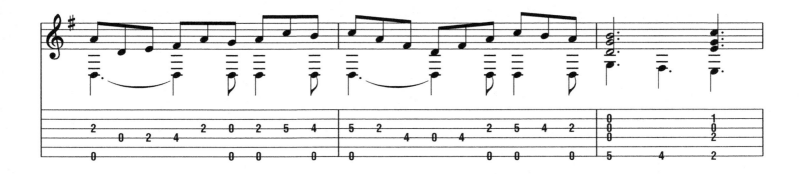

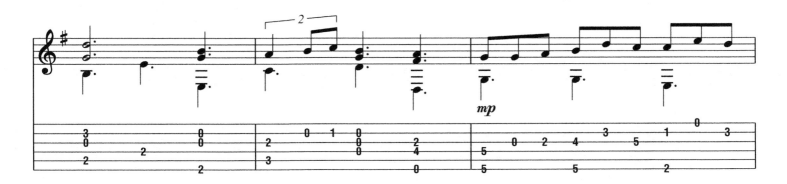

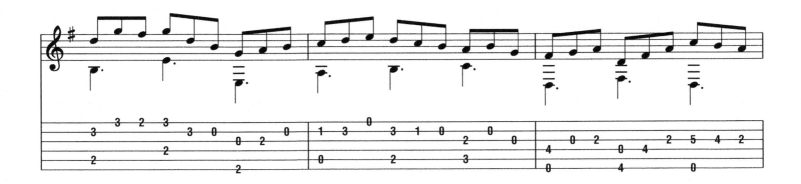

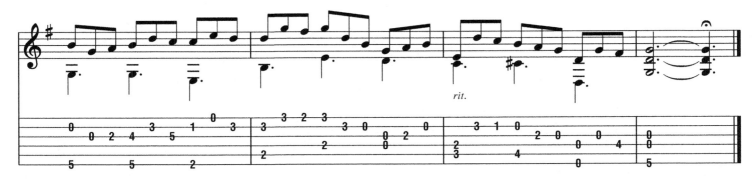

Leyenda

By Isaac Albeniz

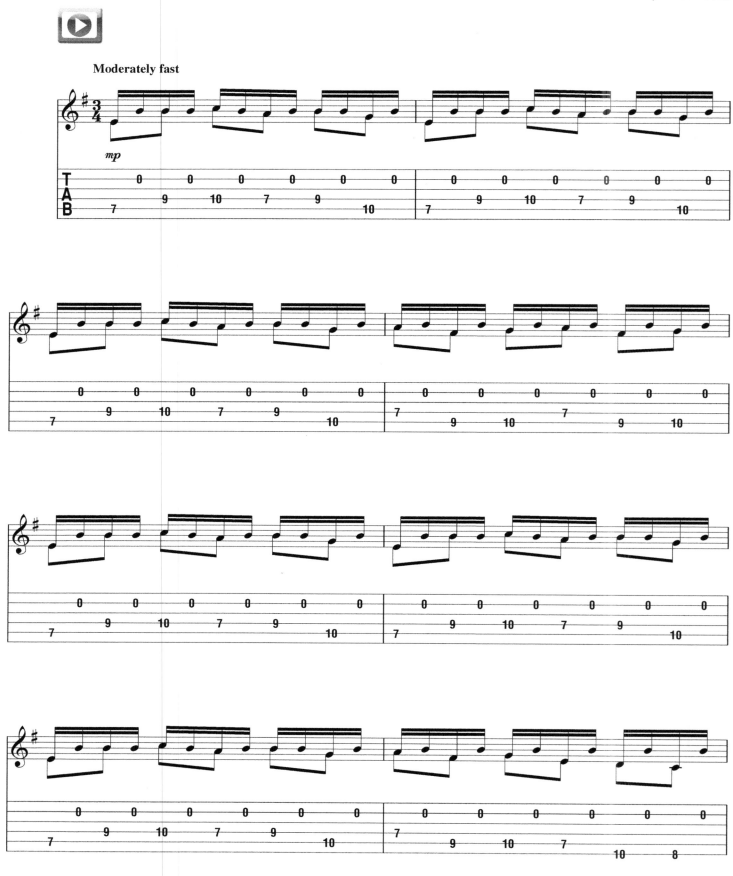

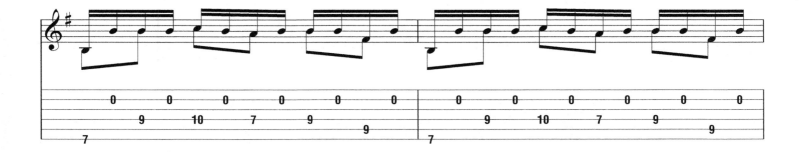

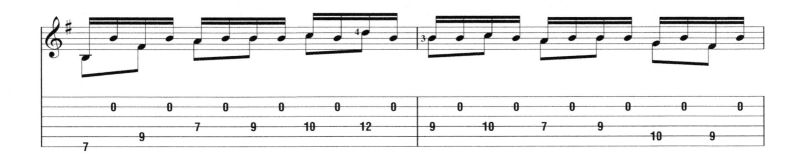

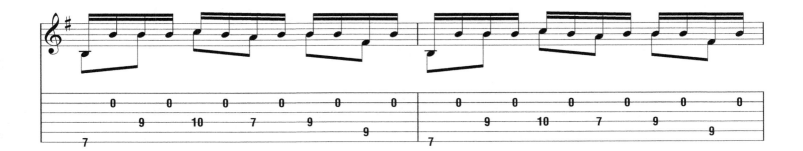

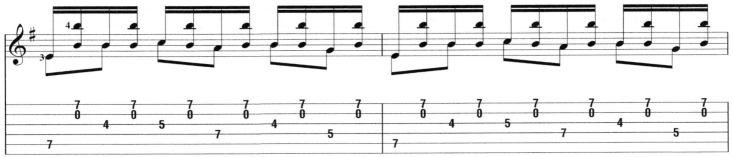

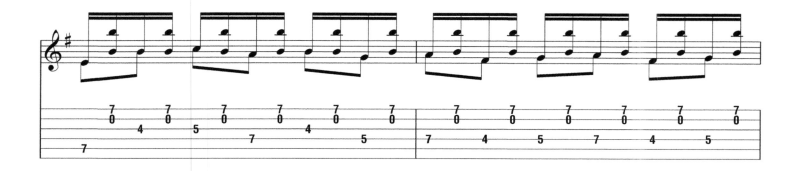

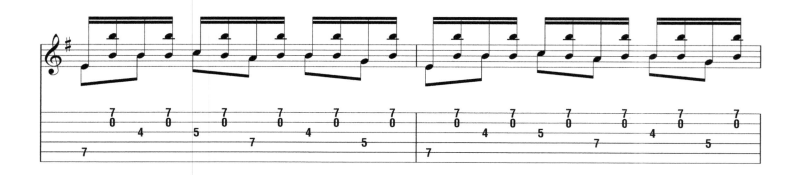

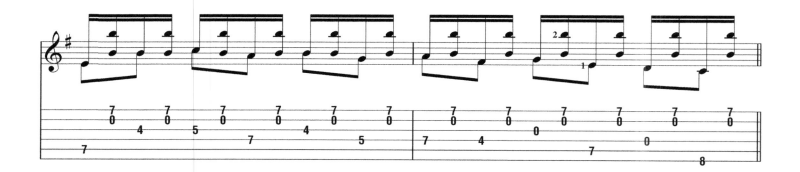

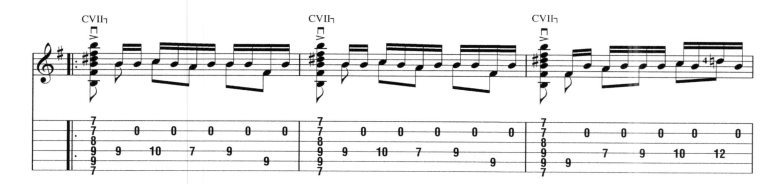

Malagueña

By Francisco Tarrega

Minuet in G
from the *Anna Magdalena Notebook* (originally for keyboard)

Johann Sebastian Bach

Moderately fast

Romance

Anonymous

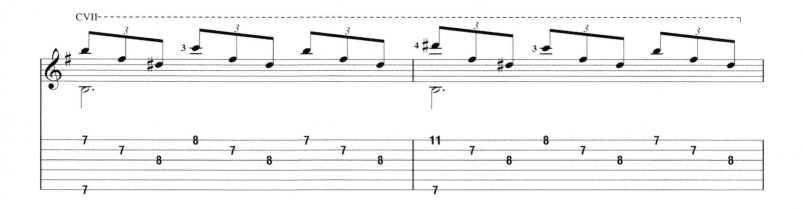

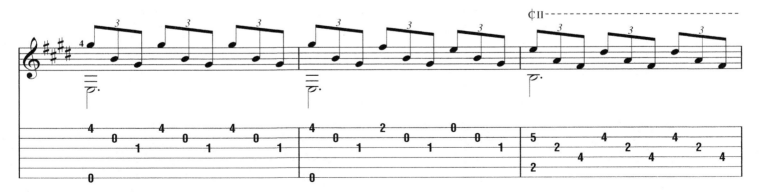

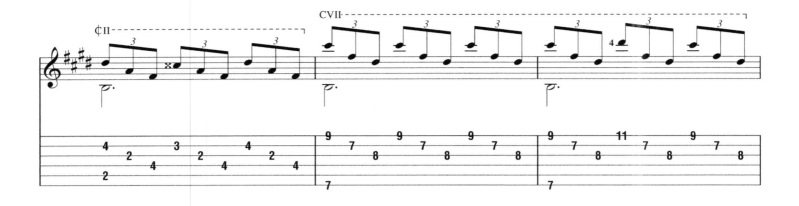

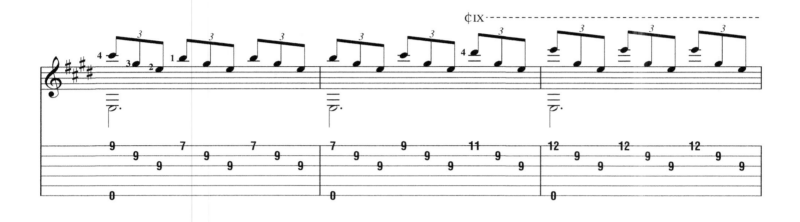

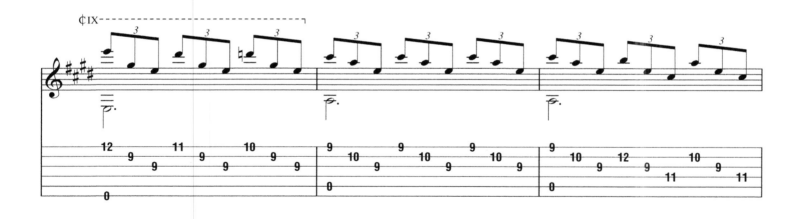

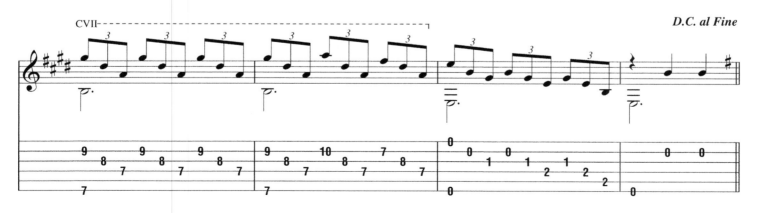

Air on the G String
from *Orchestral Suite No. 3*

Johann Sebastian Bach

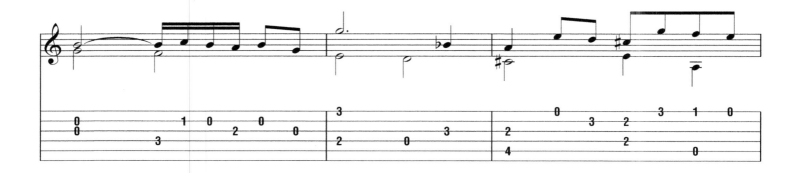

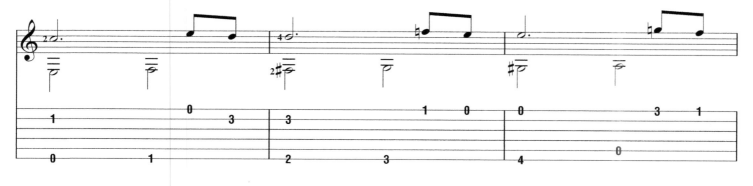

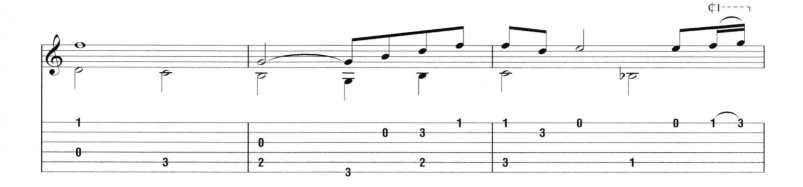

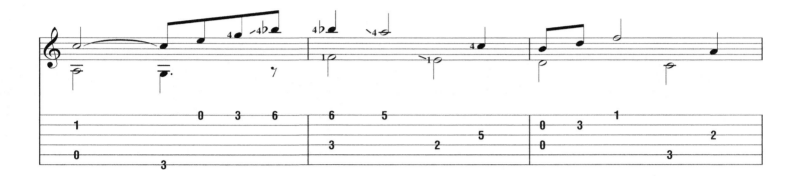

Ase's Death
from *Peer Gynt*

Edvard Grieg

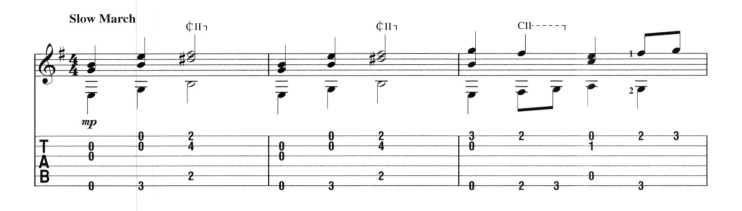

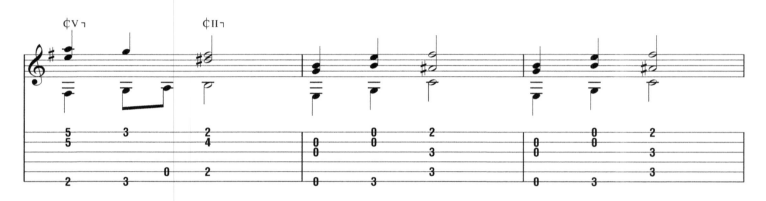

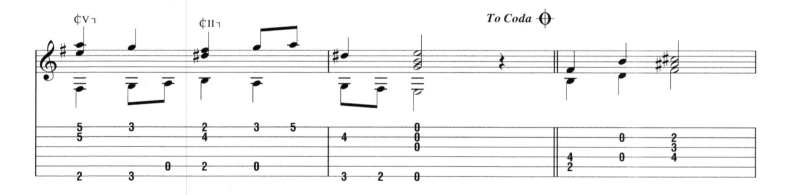

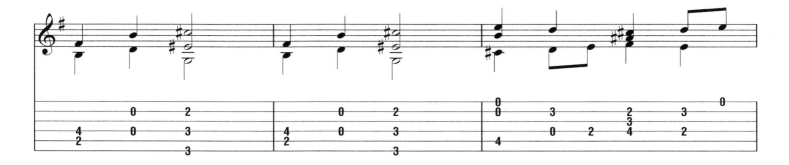

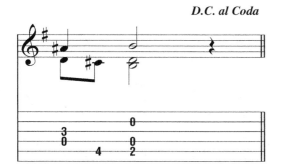

D.C. al Coda

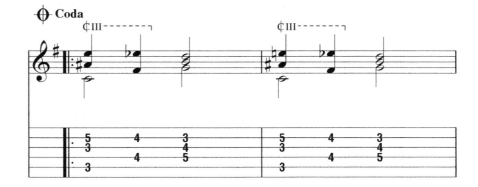

Coda

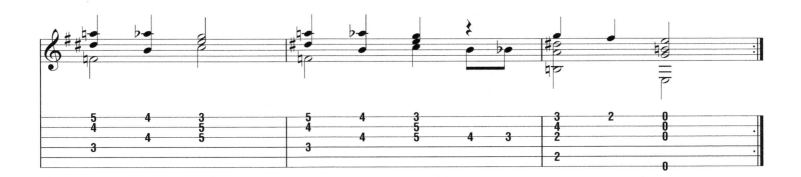

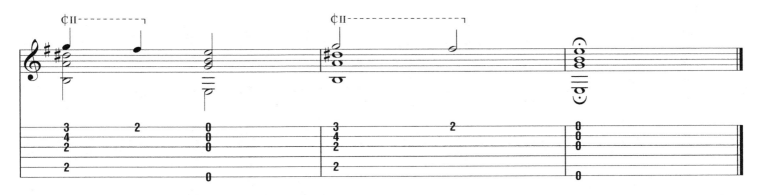

Canon in D

Johann Pachelbel

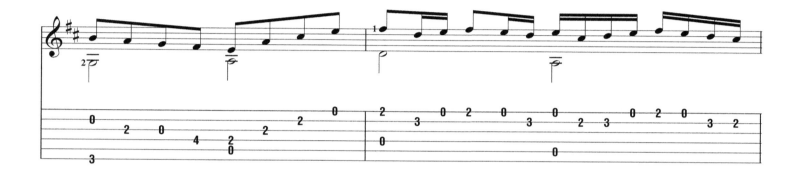

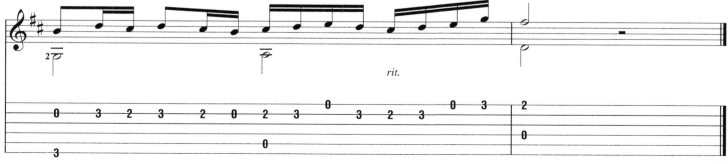

Evening Prayer
from *Hansel and Gretel*

Engelbert Humperdinck

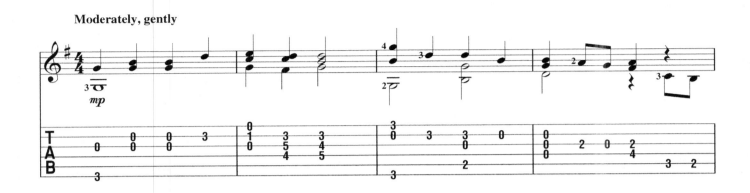

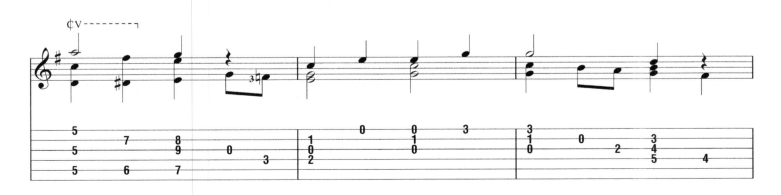

Harmonious Blacksmith

George Frideric Handel

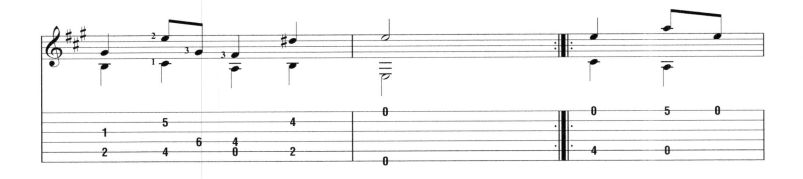

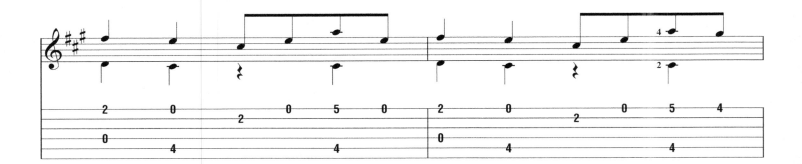

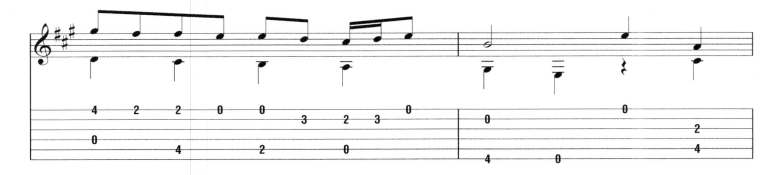

Intermezzo
from *Cavalleria rusticana*

Pietro Mascagni

Moderately slow

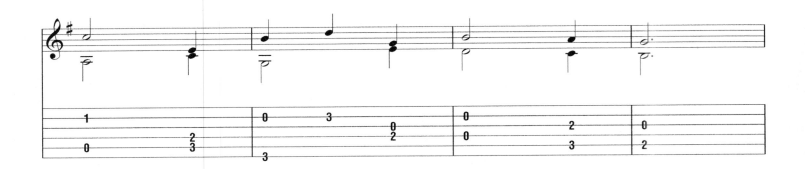

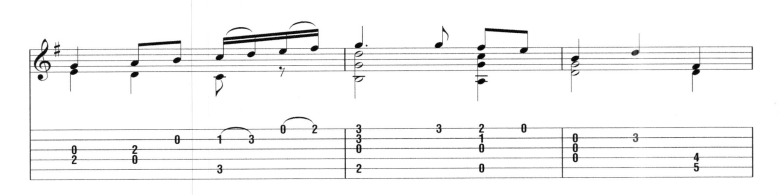

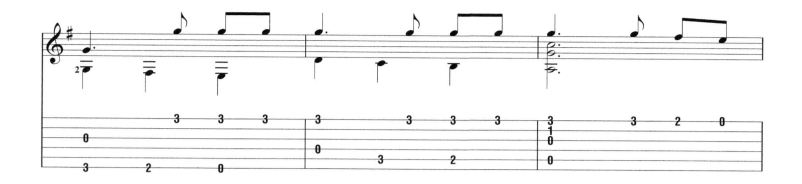

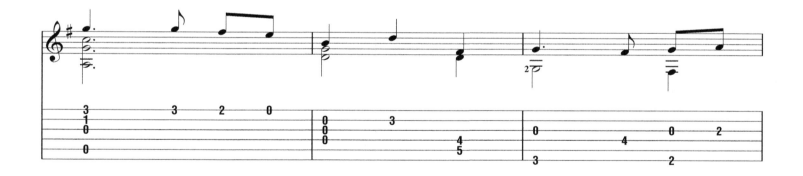

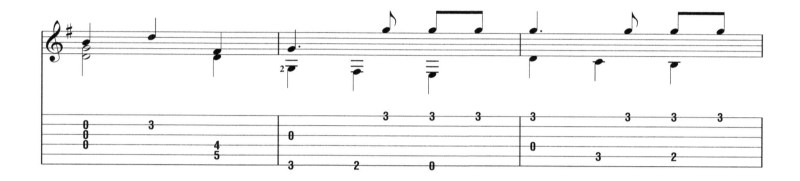

Lagrima

Francisco Tarrega

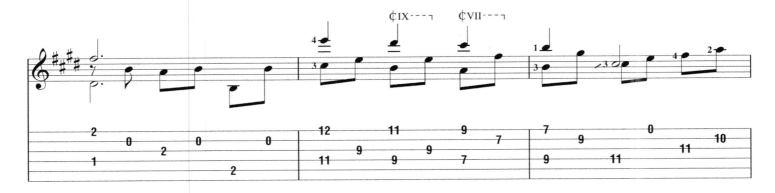

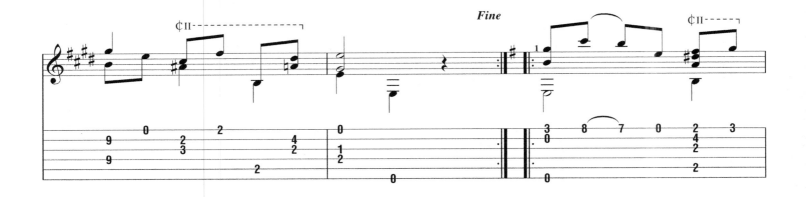

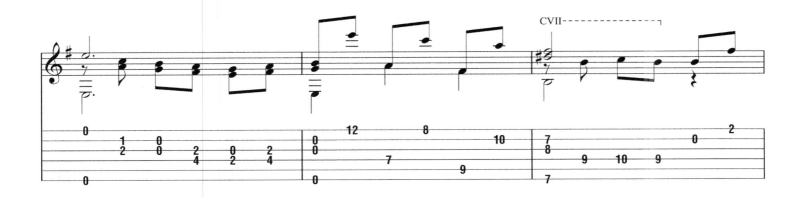

Dance of the Sugar Plum Fairy
from *The Nutcracker*

Pyotr Il'yich Tchaikovsky

Ode to Joy
from *Symphony No. 9*

Ludwig van Beethoven

Panis Angelicus

Cesar Franck

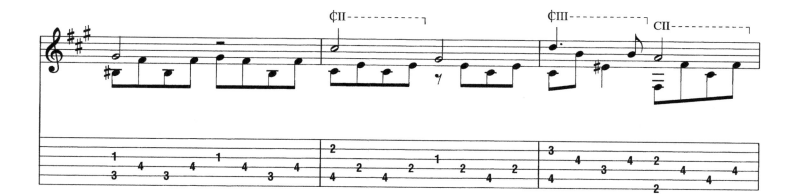

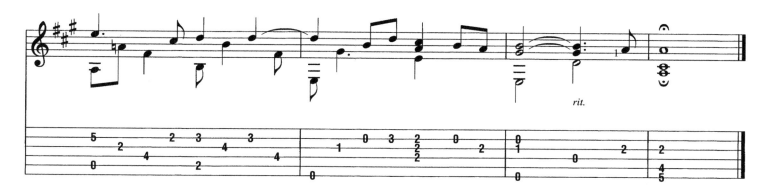

Rondeau

Jean-Joseph Mouret

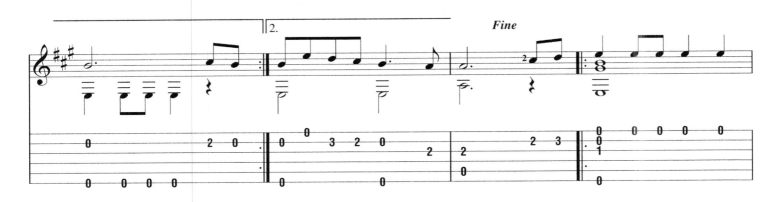

Spring
from *The Four Seasons*

By Antonio Vivaldi

Study in A

Matteo Carcassi

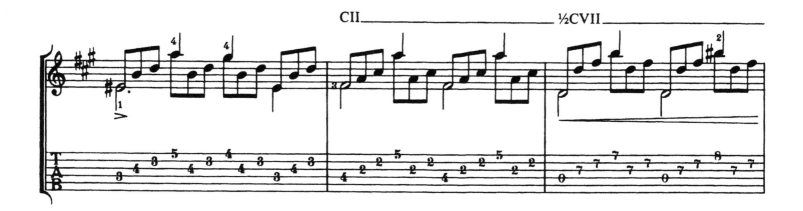

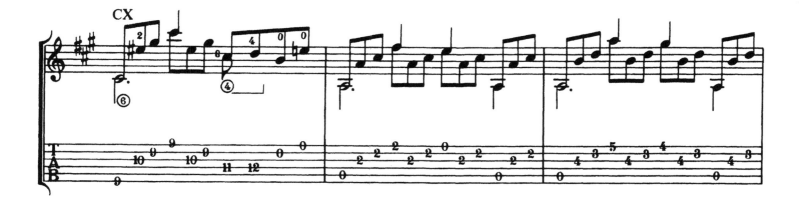

Study in B Minor

Fernando Sor

Moderato

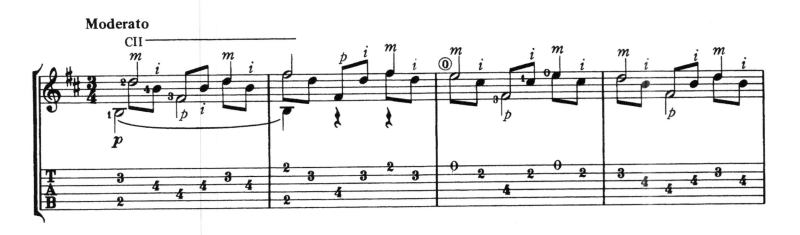

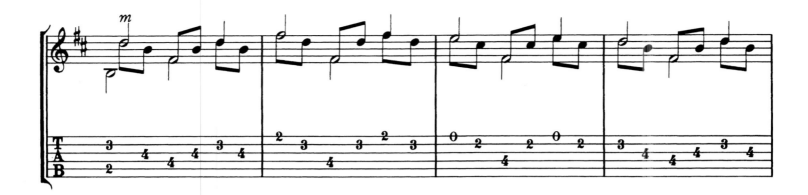

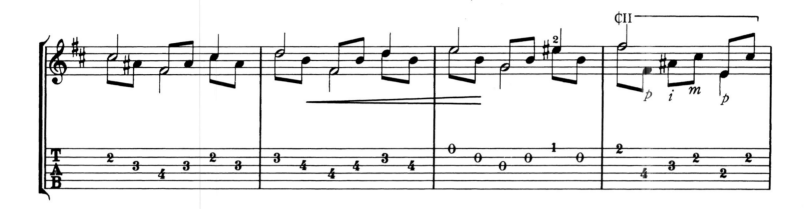

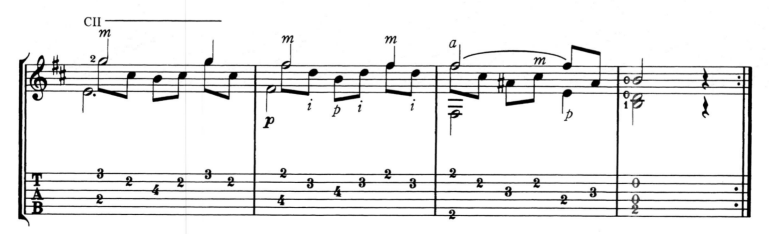